Terms and Conditions

LEGAL NOTICE

Table Of Contents

Foreword

With the increasing stress levels in life due to workplace stress, natural disasters, higher cost of livings, economic downturns and pandemic diseases, people are continuously looking for more forms of peace and comfort through various therapeutic methods.

One of the most sought after forms of therapies is Psychotherapy. Psychotherapy is a broad term used to describe a variety of counseling methods used to improve an individual's sense of wellbeing or problems in living.

Over the years, many newer and effective Psychotherapy methods have been developed and widely practice; bring a new sense of hope to the troubles faced in the world.

This guide to Psychotherapy will give you some insights as to the different types of Psychotherapies used to help people improve their lives.

Heal Yourself With Psychotherapy

Learn About The Healing Power Of Psychotherapy

Chapter 1:

Introduction To Psychotherapy

Synopsis

Psychotherapy is typically administered by a qualified clinical psychologist to a patient and involves using of various methods based on experiential relationship building, dialogue, communication and behavior change that are designed to improve mental health or well being.

A Little Background

Sometimes, it involves the intervention of other trained practitioners in the psychology and medical field such as psychiatrists, marriage counselors, hypnotherapists and even mental health counselors.

In many countries, the standards of practice are governed by a professional board of psychotherapists to ensure the level of standards applied to help patients and clients are at an acceptable level.

The most common form of technique applied by psychotherapists is the spoken conversation model. Patients are typically rested comfortably in a room, lying in a bed and put into a therapeutic environment called the "Frame" where they can freely and comfortably share their deepest personal thoughts and experiences without fear.

Psychotherapist will attempt to talk to the patient in order to facilitate the healing or self-realization process. Sometimes, the use of various other forms of communication such as the written word, artwork, drama, narrative story or music can be used to help the process.

If needed, other parties can be brought into the frame such as family members, friends or partners to help facilitate the process. This process is known as group counseling.

The type of counseling ultimately depends on the patient's diagnosis and circumstances which would affect the type of method used to successfully treat the client.

Chapter 2:

Types Of Psychotherapies

Synopsis

Today, many new types of psychotherapies have been developed, improved on and used in the clinical setting. Currently, there are up to hundreds of psychotherapeutic approaches or schools of thought.

Sorts

It was reported that by 1980 there were more than 250 types of methods used. By 1996 there were more than 450. The development of new and hybrid approaches continues around the wide variety of theoretical backgrounds and patient settings.

Many healthcare practitioners use a variety of methods based on their patients' needs. With the development of newer and more effective methods, regulatory boards have also flourished to monitor and regulate the practice of these methods to ensure the safety and effectiveness of the patients.

If you are facing a particular problem, you may consider doing your own research into the types of psychotherapies to see which would be most appropriate to help you solve your problems.

Some of the common psychotherapies used include:
- Psychoanalysis
- Gestalt Therapy
- Cognitive Behavioral Therapy
- Expressive Therapy
- Hypnotherapy

In the next chapter, we will have a more detailed look into these therapies.

Chapter 3:

Psychoanalysis

Synopsis

This technique was first developed by the father of psychoanalysis - Austrian neurologist Sigmund Freud in the 19th and early 20th century.

Here are the basic concepts of psychoanalysis:

The Concept

-Human behavior is largely due to emotional drives instead of logical drives

-These drives are largely not conscious

-Bringing these drives to awareness brings up resistance (in many forms)

-Besides genetic factors, our childhood environment affects ones development

- Conflicts between conscious view of reality and unconscious (repressed) material can result in mental illnesses such as clinical depression, anxiety etc.

- Liberation from the effects of the unconscious material is achieved through bringing this material into the consciousness

This is often portrayed in the mainstream media – where you see someone lying on a sofa chair while being counseled by someone.

It is believed that a person's verbalized thoughts, free associations, fantasies and dreams lies the key to the causes of the patient's problems, and interpretation of these findings can help the patient to create insight to the resolution of the problem.

Treatment begins when a patient fully trusts in the psychotherapist to allow him/her to analyze his problems. The patient is fully rested on a sofa couch out of sight of the psychotherapist.

From there, the psychotherapist will begin to interpret the patient's unconscious conflicts which interfere with his current days function. Through frame therapy, he is able to help the patient resolve conflicts within himself by dwelling deep into the distorted perceptions of the patient towards reality (which is mainly caused by childhood experiences).

When well rested on the couch, the patient is able to remember more clearly about his past as well as experience more resistance and transference, and be able to reorganize thoughts after the development of new insights.

Some of the common treatable problems through this method include:

Phobias, compulsions, obsessions, anxiety, attacks, depressions, sexual dysfunctions, a wide variety of relationship problems.

The patient must first undergo a preliminary stage of psychoanalysis to see if he is suited for assessment and also allow the psychotherapist to form the best model of treatment for the patient.

Chapter 4:

Gestalt Therapy

Synopsis

Gestalt therapy was founded by Fritz Perls, Laura Perls and Paul Goodman in the 1940s and 1950s.

Gestalt therapists help patients by focusing on what's happening now rather than what has happened in the past, what could be happening in the future or what should be happening.

One Approach

The emphasis is on personal responsibility, and that focuses upon the individual's experience in the present moment. Patients are thought how to enhance their awareness on the present moment rather than what they perceive or distinguish based on their pre-existing values.

Basic concepts:

1) The Phenomenological Perspective

This concept helps patients realize what is really happening in the present rather than what they perceive is happening based on their past beliefs or experiences by enhancing their state or ability of awareness.

2) The Field Theory Perspective

This theory states that parts are in immediate relationship and responsive to each other and no part is uninfluenced by what goes on elsewhere in the field.

The field replaces the notion of discrete, isolated particles. The person in his or her life space constitutes a field.
In field theory no action is at a distance; that is, what has effect must touch that which is affected in time and space.

3) The Existential Perspective

The existential perspective focuses on people's existence and relations with each other such joys and suffering. It states that people are always remaking or discovering themselves.

There is no essence of human nature to be discovered "once and for all." There are always new horizons, new problems and new opportunities.

4) The Dialogue

This method focuses on the relationship between the therapist and the patient. Gestalt therapy helps clients develop their own support for desired contact or withdrawal. Support, here means anything that makes contact or withdrawal possible such as energy, body support, breathing, information, concern for others, language etc.

Support mobilizes resources for contact or withdrawal. For example, to support the excitement accompanying contact, a person must take in enough oxygen.

The practitioner works by engaging in dialogue rather than by manipulating the patient toward some therapeutic goal. This contact is characterized by straight forward caring, warmth, acceptance and self-responsibility.

Chapter 5:

Cognitive Behavioural Therapy

Synopsis

Cognitive Behavioral Therapy (CBT) spurred from the marriage of two sub-psychotherapeutic schools to studies – Cognitive therapy and Emotive Behavioral Therapy.

The premise is this – Our thoughts affect our circumstances, not external events such as people and situations.

Behavior

CBT aims to empower a person by teaching him to adopt positive and empowering beliefs to replace his negative emotions through a systematic, goal oriented approach.

Studies have shown that his method was been able to product the fastest results ala "Instant relief". However, long term therapy is needed to produce long lasting effects.

This method can be used to treat a wide variety of diseases such as Post Traumatic Stress Disorder, eating disorders, depressions, anxiety and even panic attacks.

Cognitive Therapy

This method seeks to help the patient overcome difficulties by identifying and changing dysfunctional thinking, behavior patterns, and emotional responses.

The practitioner helps patients develop skills for changing their beliefs, identifying distorted ways of thinking and relating to others in different ways. By employing these techniques they are able to change their behaviors.

The treatment is often a non-pharmacological one, and is based on the collaboration between the patient and therapist on testing beliefs and assumptions.

For example, helping one identify how certain of one's usually unquestioned thoughts are distorted, unrealistic and unhelpful. Once those thoughts have been challenged, one's feelings about the subject matter of those thoughts are more easily subjected to change.

Behavioral Therapy

This is a learning theory which aims to treat psychopathology through techniques designed to reinforce desired and eliminate undesired behaviors

For example, let's say you are afraid of going to expensive restaurants with fancy wine glasses because you are afraid of tipping one over. The therapist will encourage you or even go together with you to a similar restaurant and tell you to deliberately tip a glass over.

You will then realize that there is actually no harm in doing so, thus deleting your previous limiting belief towards expensive wine glasses and empowering you with a new belief.

The simple act of facing your fear can have a significant outcome in changing your past beliefs and behaviors.

Chapter 6:

Expressive Therapy

Synopsis

This method is also known as expressive arts therapy or creative arts therapy. The basis of this therapy is that the process of creation can be a form of healing.

Using Arts

Unlike traditional art expression, the focus is on the creation process rather than the end product. There are several types of expressive arts therapies such as:

- Art therapy
- Dance therapy
- Drama therapy
- Music therapy
- Writing therapy

Through creative expression and tapping to one's imagination, a person can better examine his or her emotions, feelings and body. It is often used in combination with other psychotherapy methods.

Expressive arts therapy is all about the practice of using imagery, storytelling, dance, music, drama, poetry, movement, dream work, and visual arts together in a holistic way to foster human growth, development, and healing.

It is all about patients reclaiming their innate human capacity as for creative expression of individual and collective human experiences in an artistic form.

Chapter 7:

Hypnotherapy

Synopsis

Hypnotherapy is used by hypnotherapists to help patients achieve their healing goals by putting in a state of hypnosis so that they can better tap into their subconscious mind.

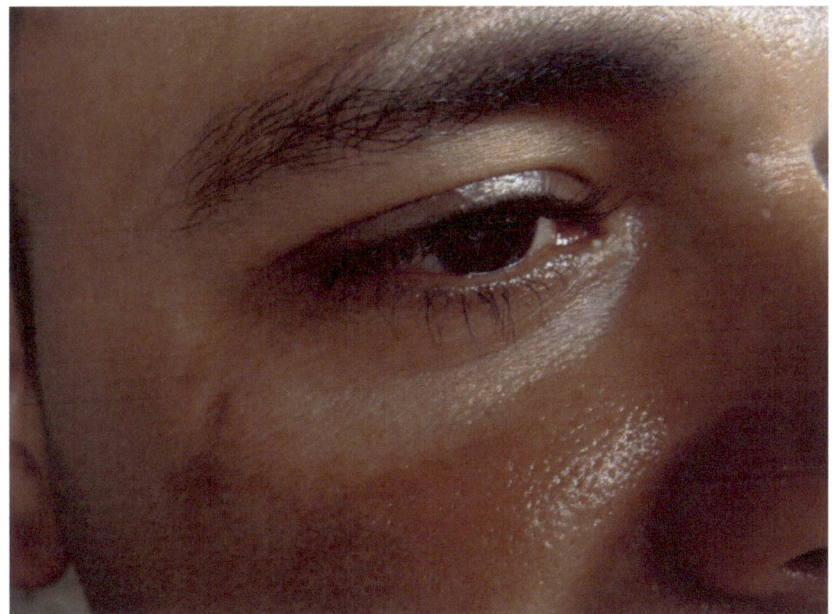

Help Thru Hypnosis

It can be used to treat a wide variety of disorders such as:
-Depression
-Anxiety
-Eating Disorders
-Sleep Disorders
-Addictions
-Post Traumatic Stress

Patients are put into a pseudo-sleep state which allows them to access their subconscious mind better. From there the hypnotherapist can suggest new beliefs and ways of thinking which empower the patient. This process is known as suggestion.

During the hypnosis stage, the relaxed state helps them to think better and realize how their past behaviors and beliefs can actually affect their current behavior.

Through suggestion and therapy, as they rehearse the new ways they want to think and feel, they lay the groundwork for changes in their future action in more empowering ways.

Today, self-hypnosis tools are commonplace such as with the use of audio cds and mp3s which can be put into a music player for self relaxation.

Wrapping Up

In short, the many different psychotherapy models have evolved over the years and have a wide range of applications in treating various psychological diseases.